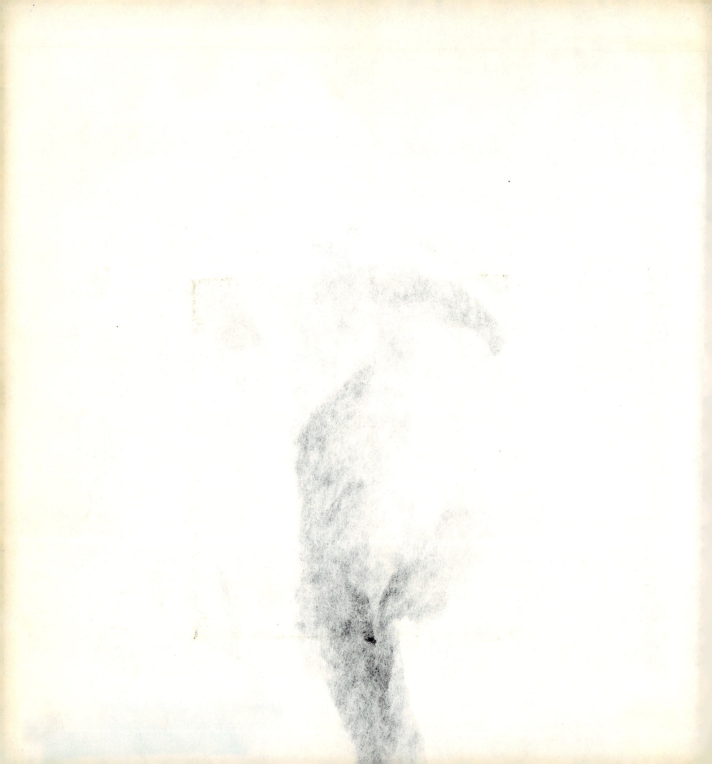

Crabs

Donna Bailey and Christine Butterworth

Steck-Vaughn
LIBRARY
A Division of Steck-Vaughn Company

Have you ever seen a crab hiding
in a shallow pool along the beach?
Some crabs are tiny.
Others are big enough to eat,
like the one in our picture.

The pea crab is the world's smallest crab.
Its body could fit on the head of a pin!
Pea crabs live inside other shellfish.
They help keep the shellfish clean.
This pea crab is living inside a clam.

The biggest crab in the world is
the Japanese spider crab.
It can grow to 13 feet wide from the tip
of one leg to the tip of the other leg!

Most crabs have a wide, flat body
with a hard outer shell.
The shell protects the crab's head and body.

A crab has five pairs of legs which grow from underneath its body.
The crab uses its legs for catching food, walking, and swimming.

A crab has one pair of legs with big claws for catching and holding its food.
The crab also uses these claws to fight its enemies.

Most crabs have a pair of legs shaped like paddles.
The crab uses these legs for swimming.
Some crabs have a small tail under their bodies to help them swim.

A crab spends most of its day eating.
It has long feelers to help it find food.
Its eyes are on stalks on top of its head
so the crab can see all around.

Crabs have different ways of talking
to one another.
Some wave their claws in the air.
Others drum their claws on the ground.

When a crab is afraid or angry,
it waves its claws and
makes itself look very fierce.

This robber crab digs
a burrow for protection.
It uses its claws to chip open
coconuts for food.
When it is time to mate, the
robber crab crawls to the sea.

Most kinds of crabs mate in salt water.
The female carries more than
a million eggs under her belly.
She holds them in place with her tail.

When the eggs hatch, a tiny grub called
a larva comes out of each egg.
A crab larva changes its shape
many times before it grows to look
like the parent crabs.

As a young crab grows, it gets
too big for its shell.
Then it crawls out of the old shell.
Its shiny new skin hardens
to make another shell.

Most crabs live in the sea.
This is a freshwater crab.
It feeds on weeds and small fish
in the rivers.

Some crabs live on land.
This robber crab has huge, strong claws.
It climbs up coconut palms and uses
its claws to make a hole in the hard,
outer shell of a coconut.
Then it eats the soft, white flesh inside.

These small land crabs live on Christmas Island in the Pacific Ocean. Once a year, they leave their burrows and walk to the sea.

The crabs need to mate in seawater, so millions of them swarm over the ground towards the shore.
The crabs even go through the houses and over tennis courts to get to the ocean!

Millions of crabs swarm down the cliffs and into the sea where they mate.
Then the crabs begin the long march back to their burrows.

This fiddler crab lives on
sandy beaches or muddy shores.

It digs a burrow for itself in the sand. The burrow is cool and damp and protects the crab from the hot sun.

The male fiddler crab has one
very large front claw.
When he waves it in the air, it looks
like someone playing a fiddle.
That's how the crab got its name.

These two male crabs are fighting with their big front claws.
If a crab's claw breaks off during a fight, a new claw will grow again in the same place.

Crabs have different ways of hiding from their enemies.
This crab has buried itself in the mud.
It pokes one eye above the mud to see if it is safe to come out.

This spider crab hides by sticking seaweed onto the hooks on its back. It changes the weed to match the color of the other weeds around it.

Sponge crabs have a very clever way of hiding.

First, the sponge crab cuts a piece of living sponge with its claws.

Then the crab holds the sponge on its back with its last two pairs of legs.
The sponge keeps growing and makes a shelter for the crab.

Hermit crabs make their homes in empty shells.
A hermit crab has a long, soft body.
It needs the shell to protect it.

This hermit crab lives inside
the empty shell of a sea snail.
The hermit crab's tiny back legs
hold on tight to the inside of the shell.

When a hermit crab goes inside the shell to hide, it closes the mouth of the shell with its big front claw.

The hermit crab drags the shell
around with it when it walks.
When it grows too big for the shell,
the crab must look for a bigger one.

Index

bodies 5, 8
burrows 18, 20, 22
Christmas Island 18–20
clam 3
claws 7, 10, 11, 23, 24, 27, 31
coconuts 17
eggs 13, 14
eyes 9, 15
fear 11
feelers 9
female crab 12, 13
fiddler crabs 21–24
fighting 7, 24
food 6, 7, 17
freshwater crab 16
head 5, 9
hermit crabs 29–32
hiding 25–28, 31
Japanese spider crab 4

land crabs 17–20
larva 14
legs 4, 6–8, 12, 28, 30
male crab 12
mating 12, 19, 20
pea crab 3
pool 2
robber crab 17
rocks 2
seaweed 26
shellfish 3
shells 5, 15, 29, 30
spider crab 26
sponge crabs 27, 28
swimming 6, 8
tail 8, 13
talking 10
walking 6, 32

Reading Consultant: Diana Bentley
Editorial Consultant: Donna Bailey
Supervising Editor: Elizabeth Strauss
Project Editor: Becky Ward

Illustrated by Paula Chasty
Picture research by Jennifer Garratt
Designed by Richard Garratt Design

Photographs
Cover: Bruce Coleman (Jane Burton)
Ardea: 4 (P. Morris)
Bruce Coleman: title page (David Hughes), 2 (Martin Dohrn), 3,6,25,26,28,30,31 (Jane Burton), 7 (Neville Fox-Davies), 11 (David Hughes), 12 (Mike Price), 16 (Hans Reinhard), 21 (Gerald Cubitt), 22 (Dieter & Mary Plage), 23 (Dieter Plage), 24 (C.B. Frith)
Colorific!: 18,19,20 (Roger Garwood)
OSF Picture Library: 5 (Barrie Watts), 10 (Fredrick Ehrenstrom), 13,29 (G. Bernard), 17 (Waina Cheng), 32 (Colin Milkins)

Library of Congress Cataloging-in-Publication Data: Butterworth, Christine. Crabs / Christine Butterworth and Donna Bailey. p. cm.—(Animal world) Includes index. SUMMARY: Explores the world of crabs, from the tiny pea crab to the large Japanese spider crab, explaining how crabs use their claws and legs for catching food, walking, and swimming.   ISBN 0-8114-2640-8   1. Crabs—Juvenile literature.   [1. Crabs.]   I. Bailey, Donna. II. Title.   III. Series: Butterworth, Christine. Animal world.   QL444.M33B88   1990   595.3'842—dc20   90-36168   CIP   AC

ISBN 0-8114-2640-8
Copyright 1991 Steck-Vaughn Company
Original copyright Heinemann Children's Reference 1991
All rights reserved. No part of the material protected by this copyright may be reproduced or utilized in any form or by any means, electronic or mechanical, including photocopying, recording, or by any information storage and retrieval system, without permission in writing from the copyright owner. Requests for permission to make copies of any part of the work should be mailed to: Copyright Permissions, Steck-Vaughn Company, P.O. Box 26015, Austin, Texas 78755. Printed in the United States of America.

2 3 4 5 6 7 8 9 0 LB 96 95 94 93 92